Zini's Kaleidoscope

Written and Illustrated by
Ashley M. Matson

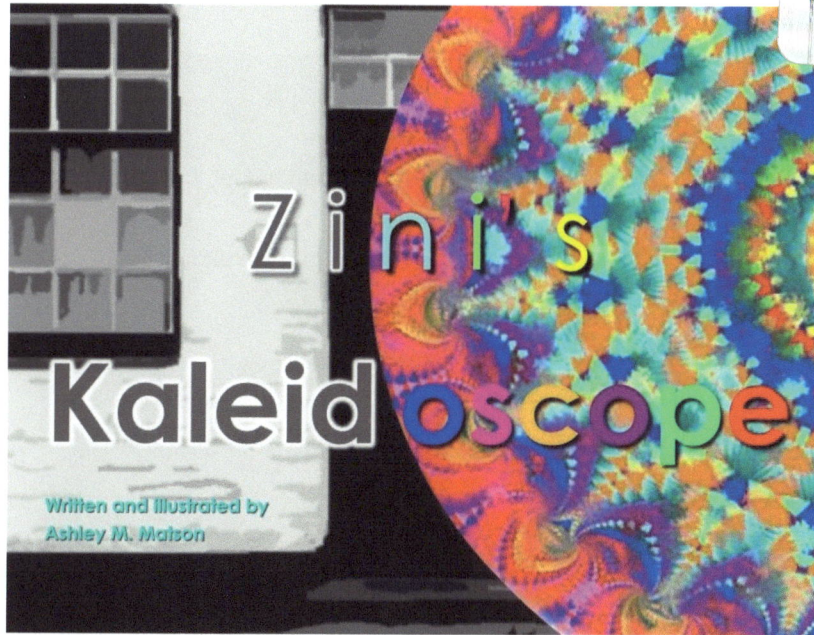

To Sean Ellis Sutton and Christina Michele Sutton for being the color in my world. Thank you for your unconditional love, constant encouragement, and endless inspiration.

To my mom, Barbie Matson, and my dad, Ricky Matson, for teaching me how to twist my kaleidoscope so long ago. Thank you for pointing out every silver lining — including the one in me.

Name pronunciation:

Zini: Zee-nee

Makeda: Mah-KAI-dah

Glossary of names:

Wazinia: (origin — Swahili) open mind

Makeda: (origin — Ethiopic) greatness; the beautiful

Attributions:

kaleidoscope, building, school, home: www.pixabay.com

kaleidoscope design: site-http://helpsoft.ru/artscope/en/

"Z! Time to get up!"

The cold, heavy darkness blanketed Zini. It was Tuesday morning. He could hear his mom getting ready for work, calling from the only other room.

"Come on, baby. I am going to have to leave soon. You need to hurry to the bus stop to make it on time. You know it won't wait, so get up, get dressed, and come eat this cereal."

Zini squinted in the dark, snuggled deep into their shared mattress. Momma didn't have to call loud for him to hear.

1

It was so hard to get out of his nestled spot, but he found the energy and forced himself up. Anything was easier than upsetting Momma early in the morning.

Zini sluggishly pulled on his clothes from a neatly folded pile and dragged himself to the table.

Everything still a little blurry, he noticed a decorative object placed next to his bowl.

Zini sat down and held it up inquisitively.

"Momma, what's this?" he asked, examining it.

"Oh, that's a kaleidoscope. I saw it in the thrift store window for a dollar while I was walking home. I got it for you. I had one when I was little. Look in it, and twist this end," she pointed.

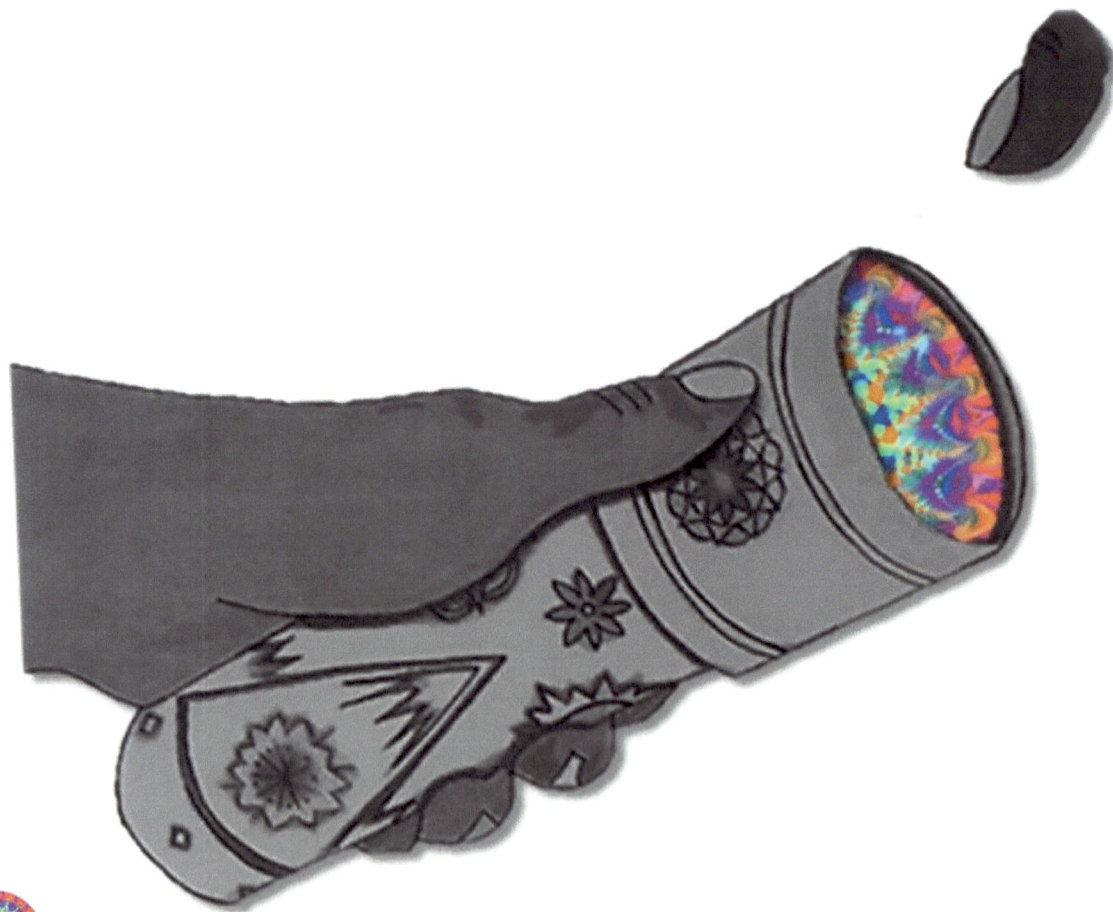

Zini brought it close to his eye and couldn't believe what he saw! There were so many beautiful colors and brilliant shapes! It was like magic!

4

"Alright Z, come on," Momma said, interrupting his admiration. "You can use it when you get home, but now you need to eat that cereal and go."

Zini remembered his bran flake cereal, but when he looked down at it through his kaleidoscope, it was every color and shape! It was like that cereal with the marshmallows he had always wanted to try.

While Momma was turned around, Zini tucked the kaleidoscope into his pocket. He knew she wouldn't want him to take it. She always warned him about distractions, but he made himself a silent promise to stay focused despite having it.

"Bye, Momma, I love you," he said, kissing her quickly on the cheek.
"I love you too. Be careful today. Make sure you do everything to learn."
"Yes ma'am, Momma," Zini replied and rushed out the door.

Zini bounded down the concrete stairs of the apartment building and out onto the street. The sun was just rising, so he could make out a few silhouettes as he walked.

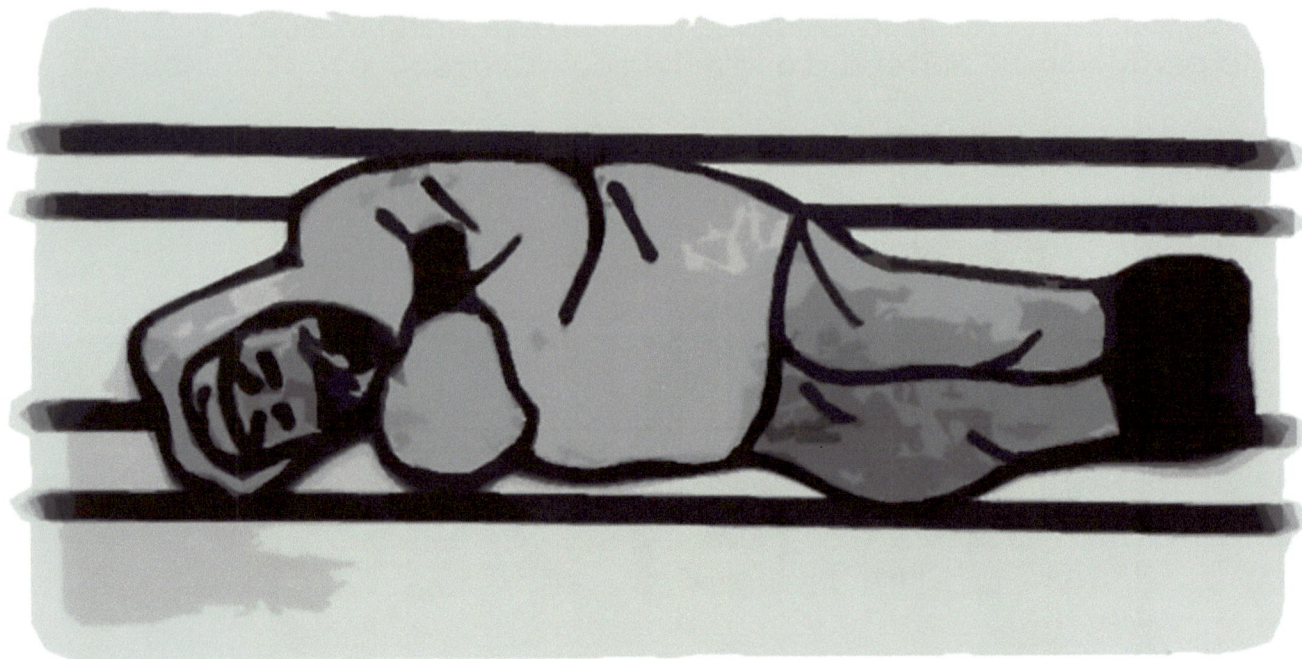

One was Mr. Benny, still sleeping on the bench from the night before. He was shivering slightly and making little grunt noises. Zini wondered what he saw as he slept.

Zini kept up his pace, but moved quietly, allowing Mr. Benny to rest.

He got to the corner where Jamal always stood scowling, pivoting his head, scanning the streets, and leaning against the post.

Zini nodded timidly to him, diverted his eyes, and hurried to turn up the next street. Jamal remained stoic, only shifting his glare and panning the block.

Zini made it to the city bus stop just as the bus was pulling up. He paused to turn back toward his neighborhood. Still gray with smog, he could faintly see the gutter of the apartment building hanging down toward the cracked sidewalk. The dark figures lingered.

Zini pulled the kaleidoscope up to his eye. The transformation was amazing! His building was like a palace covered in magnificent mosaics. Mr. Benny was bathed in peaceful rainbows, floating on a dream cloud. Jamal was immersed in the patterned design similar to pictures Zini had seen in a book about Italy.

The whole ride, through his kaleidoscope, Zini marvelled at the splendor of the usually monotonous sights.

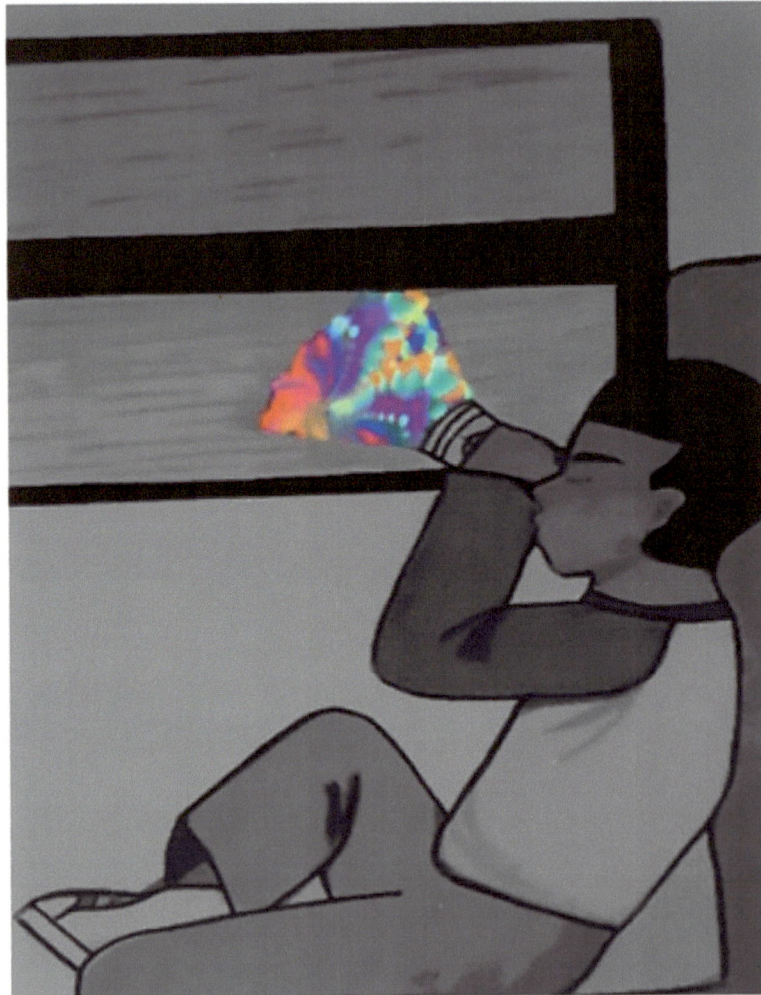

The lady shuffling on the sidewalk with her bags was a queen dressed in the finest clothes. The bits of trash strewn along the curb were gems waiting to be discovered. Even the condemned buildings with broken windows were impressive works of art.

Arriving at school, Zini tucked the kaleidoscope back into his pocket and scurried up to the building. It didn't seem like the bell had rung yet. Whew. He didn't want Momma getting a call that he was late.

Zini walked speedily, dodging obstacles, through the frenzied hallways. They were filled with children playing roughly while others yelled insults littered with bad words.

Slightly short of breath, he arrived at Ms. Makeda's class and went to his seat. She was writing their first assignment on the board and didn't notice him come in.

She was pretty and kind, but she was stern and direct. She reminded him of Momma. Ms. Makeda was the best teacher in the third grade.

She didn't ever have to take him in the hallway or put him in the corner, but that could not be said for his classmates. Zini always wished the other students would be respectful to her and listen. Instead, Ms. Makeda had to look at them with her eyebrows together so much that she was getting little lines between them.

As Ms. Makeda continued preparing for the day, Zini took out his kaleidoscope. Through that lens, her anxieties melted away, and she glowed like an angel. Smiling, he put it back in his pocket.

The bell rang, and students ran in wildly. Ms. Makeda made each one go back out and "try again." James had to try again three times.

Still a bit unruly, but better, everyone was in the class. It was time to start. Zini watched as a sort of power struggle ensued between the teacher giving concise directions and the children hurling paper objects.

Zini tried his best to listen and learn. Ms. Makeda had projected a series of cloud pictures. He studied them remembering how the sky looks after storms, wondering if that was the meaning he should make. Momma would ask him when he got home, and she wouldn't accept "nothing." He certainly couldn't blame the other kids in the class. He had to learn, so he sat patiently, searching for significance amid the chaos.

As Ms. Makeda worked to begin instruction, Zini discreetly raised his kaleidoscope to his eye. The madness was altered into a celestial scene.

The other children shimmered brightly, gliding through space, finally settling into a state of calm attentiveness. Zini was relieved. He knew that, with this change, he could absorb everything his teacher had to share. Momma would be so proud!

As the school day ended, Zini felt immense excitement about life. Grays faded as his world became a vibrant place through his kaleidoscope. He wanted to see, do, and learn more every second.

Heading home on the city bus, Zini leaned his head against the window. He was exhausted from his exhilarating day. He smiled as he rested with his eyes closed.

Suddenly, Zini felt the bus jerk. It must be his stop. He jumped up, afraid of the bus pulling off with him still on it. That happened once before, and he had to ride the whole route again, getting home so late that Momma was crying.

He safely reached the apartment steps, careful not to walk through the shattered bottles. He made a final turn to see the bus become a decorated chariot through his kaleidoscope…

WAIT! Where was his kaleidoscope?! He had left it on the bus in his rush to get off! He tried to chase after, but it was gone, leaving him in a cloud of smoke.

Tears filled his eyes as he looked around at the dismal, broken world he had returned to. Defeated, Zini trudged up the stairs.

19

Momma heard the door and greeted him. Zini mumbled a return greeting with his head still low.

"What's wrong, Z?" Momma asked.

"My kaleidoscope, Momma. It's gone. I left it on the bus. You got it for me, and I left it. I am so sorry, Momma. Please don't be mad."

Momma exhaled a long time with her lips pressed into a straight line. She crossed the tiny room to her son and put her arm around him, pulling him close.

"You know you shouldn't have taken it with you," she scolded. "You know what I say about distractions. This happens when we aren't careful. You have to take care of your things."

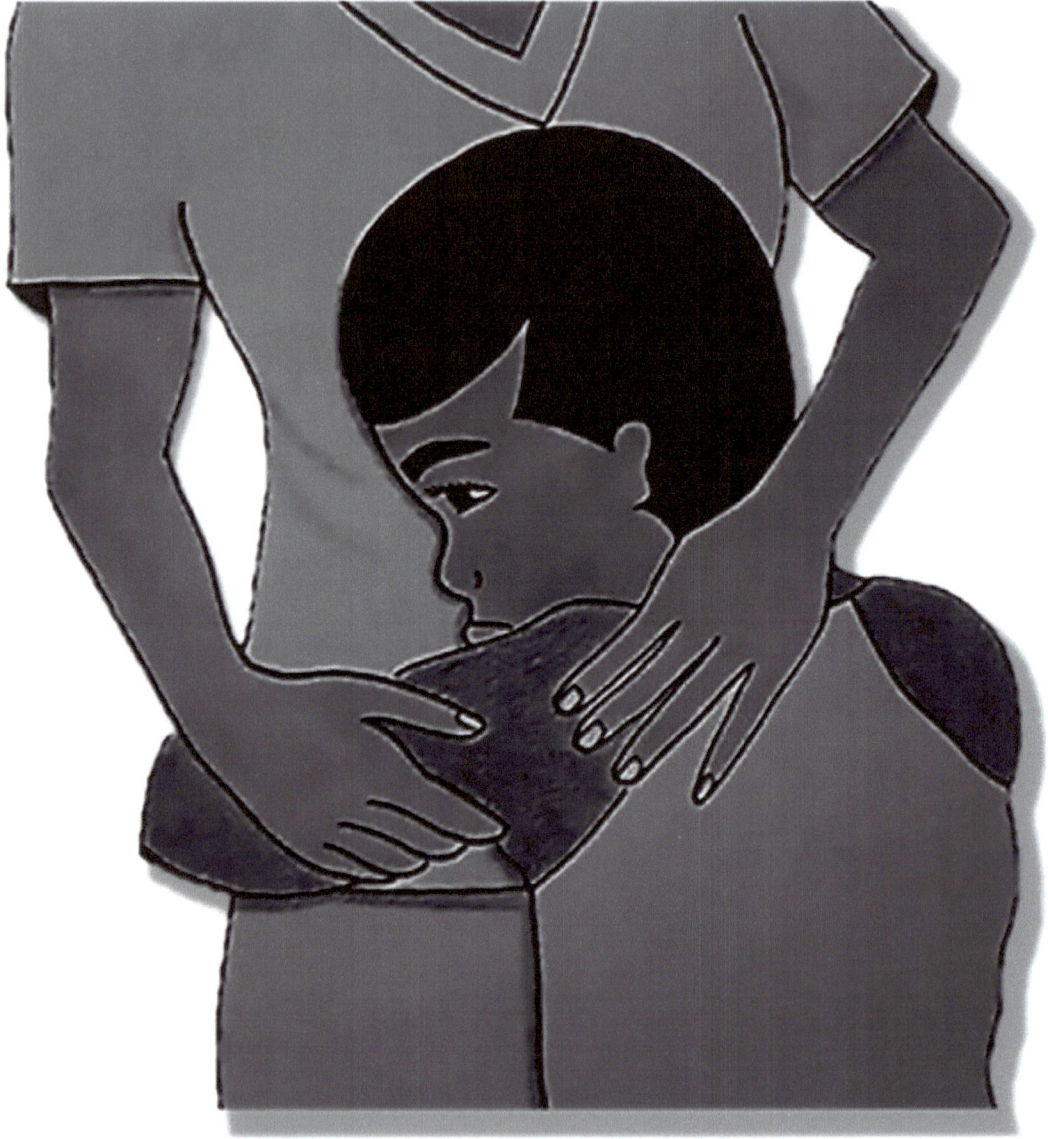

Then, Momma bent her knees in front of him so that their eyes met, and her voice grew softer.

"Pick your head up. I know you liked the kaleidoscope, but what made it so special to you?"

"It was so beautiful," Zini replied, sniffling. "It had all these bright colors and pretty shapes. It was more creative than I could imagine. It didn't matter that the little pieces weren't whole because they made anything I looked at perfect. Everything had movement and life. It took what was there... the bad stuff... and made it better. It fixed what was broken."

Momma squeezed his hands.

"Zini, do you know why I gave it to you?" she asked.
"No, ma'am," Zini responded.
"The moment I saw it, it reminded me of you, but you don't need it to fix what is broken.
You are the beauty in this world."

Momma waited a moment as a confused expression crossed Zini's face.
"Close your eyes, Zini. Think about the kaleidoscope. Can you see it?"
Zini closed his eyes tight. "Yes, Momma," he said, as a single tear crept from the corner
of his eye.

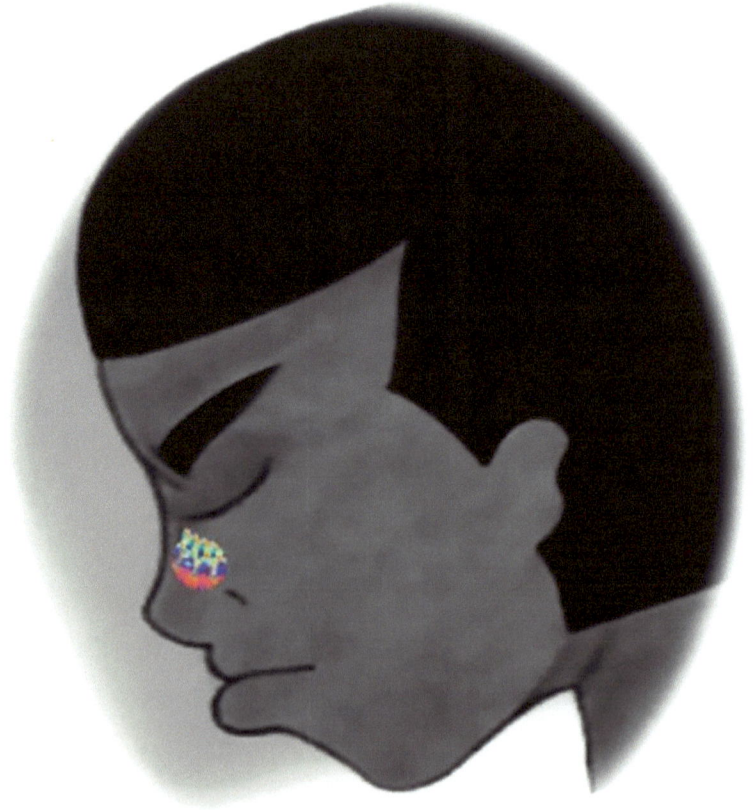

"Your spirit is the bright color," Momma began.

Zini scrunched his eyes and forehead a little tighter, trying to see. Momma waited before gently continuing.

"You see those pieces — little fragments forming brilliant shapes? That's your heart using your imagination to see the good in things — being creative and making something from nothing."

Zini stood motionless, eyes still closed, listening.

"The movement is your mind," she explained, "the way you think so deeply and search for solutions…"

Zini squinted more intently, hanging on Momma's every word.

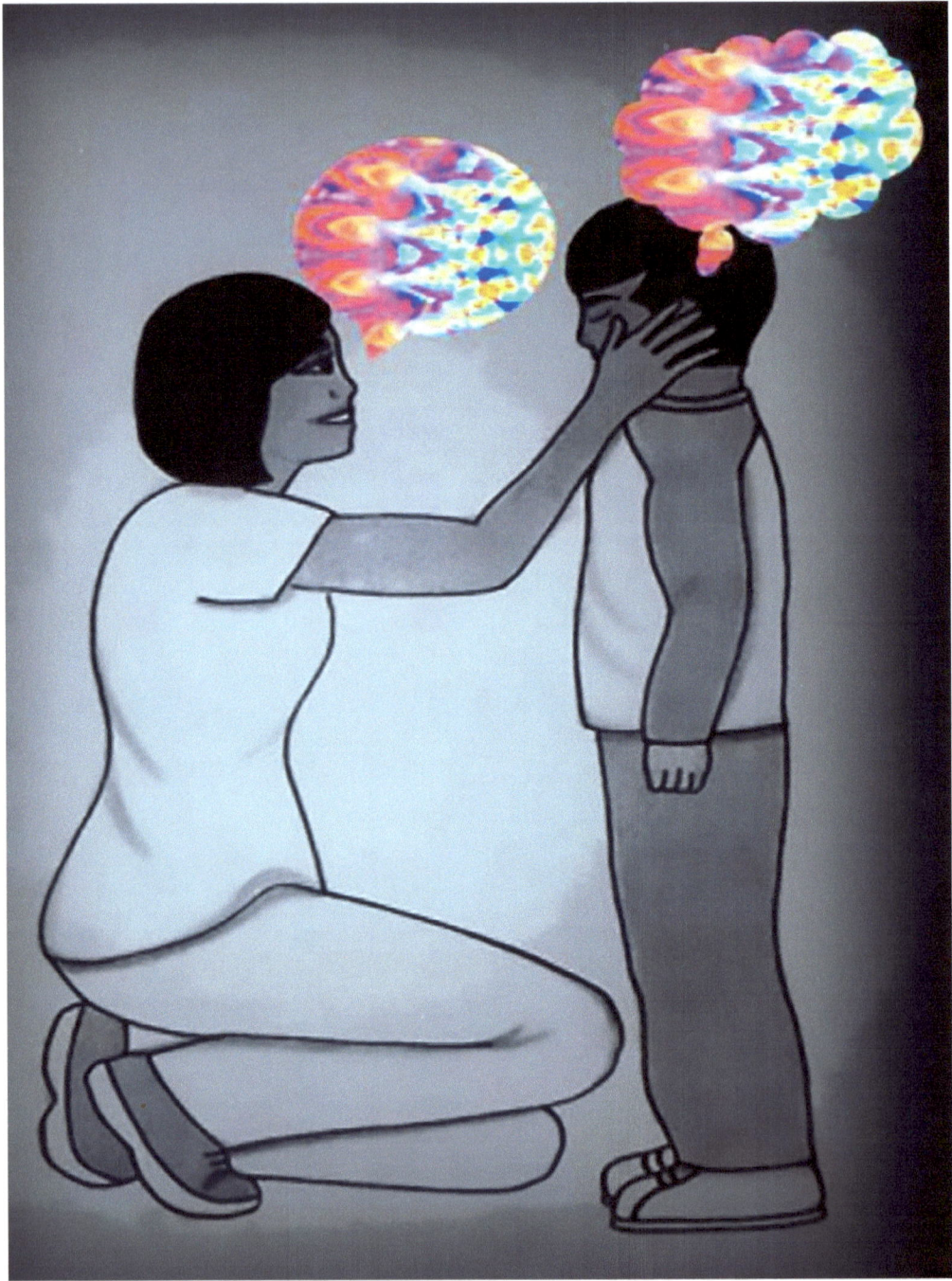

"You were using a kaleidoscope to bring color, light, creativity, and movement to this world, but Zini, my color, light, creativity, movement, and HOPE are all in you! I lived in a world of nothingness until you came. You are my kaleidoscope. Your name, Wazinia, means 'open mind' in Swahili. Don't be burdened by this world. Open yourself to all of your gifts. Your potential is infinite. Your presence radiates color, light, creativity, movement, and hope. You don't have to rely on anything else.

"Be what we need... what the world needs. Be our kaleidoscope."

In that instant, Zini opened his eyes, tears streaming, and hugged his mom. He knew what he needed to do.

The next morning, all of the typical grays gave way to gorgeous light, aura, and color.

Zini was not blind to reality, but he knew that he could be a source for good by staying true to his spirit, heart, and mind.

Each blink of Zini's eyes was like twisting his kaleidoscope. He saw what could be. He shifted his perspective and turned nothing to something. He adjusted his vision and bent grays to prisms. He analyzed issues and crafted solutions to problems. When he couldn't change situations, he decided to be a strong example of the change that was needed. He could see life just as he had through the kaleidoscope — only now, he chose to see it, but more importantly, he chose to be it.

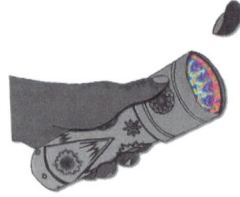

www.ingramcontent.com/pod-product-compliance
Lightning Source LLC
Chambersburg PA
CBHW041239040426

42445CB00004B/87